Ways to Go

TRAINS GO!

By John Matthew Williams

Gareth Stevens
PUBLISHING

Please visit our website, www.garethstevens.com. For a free color catalog of all our high-quality books, call toll free 1-800-542-2595 or fax 1-877-542-2596.

Cataloging-in-Publication Data
Names: Williams, John Matthew.
Title: Trains go! / John Matthew Williams.
Description: New York : Gareth Stevens Publishing, 2018. | Series: Ways to go | Includes index.
Identifiers: ISBN 9781538210253 (pbk.) | ISBN 9781538210277 (library bound) | ISBN 9781538210260 (6 pack)
Subjects: LCSH: Locomotives–Juvenile literature. | Railroad trains–Juvenile literature.
Classification: LCC TF148.W55 2018 | DDC 385–dc23

First Edition

Published in 2018 by
Gareth Stevens Publishing
111 East 14th Street, Suite 349
New York, NY 10003

Editor: Kate Mikoley
Designer: Sam DeMartin

Photo credits: Cover, p. 1 LEE SNIDER PHOTO IMAGES/Shutterstock.com; p. 5 Stephen B. Goodwin/Shutterstock.com; p. 7 Scanrail1/Shutterstock.com; p. 9 Paolo Bona/Shutterstock.com; pp. 11, 24 (track) karin claus/Shutterstock.com; pp. 13, 23 BCFC/Shutterstock.com; p. 15 (bottom) GE_4530/Shutterstock.com; p. 15 (top left) Sailorr/Shutterstock.com; p. 15 (top right) Harri Aho/Shutterstock.com; p. 17 Supannee_Hickman/Shutterstock.com; pp. 19, 24 (subway) rorem/Shutterstock.com; p. 21 Benoit Daoust/Shutterstock.com.

Printed in the United States of America

CPSIA compliance information: Batch #CW18GS: For further information contact Gareth Stevens, New York, New York at 1-800-542-2595.

Contents

Trains help us go!

Coachclass

They are very fast.

People drive trains.

ALSTOM

Trains move on a track.

Trains can pull many cars.

There are many kinds of trains.

1136

Some move people.

SOUTHWEST
CHIEF

Big cities have
special trains.
These are subways.

Exit
1

They move many
people around the city.

APEX
Choose your trade at Apex
212 675-6600
$1.89

Others move things
like food.
These things are
called freight.

Words to Know

subway

track

Index